"That's How I Roll"

moments from a life

Mary B. Harrison

Grey Hawk Books

Cover design by Sally Lunt

For Ken
February 1, 1959—December 26, 2013

To his deceased brothers, John and Scott,
and to his living brother, Chris

"Rage, rage against the dying of the light."
-Dylan Thomas

Contents

ONE

moments from a life

leaves float in the field
the *little yellow*
glides with the wind

moments from a life

Tragedy

Early summer, my son, Ken, and I sit in matching recliners and talk about his school work and plans for starting his own business. We watch, through a window, a young cottontail dash from the sweet gum toward the fence, how he moves through sun and shadow, his hind legs stirring the tall grass. How he is unaware of the red-tailed hawk shadowing.

Today, alone in the sun room, I look for another cottontail, one of a family I've been watching for weeks. The past few days—no sign of any of them. Only the red-tailed hawk sitting on the fence near the sweet gum, the tree's green pointed leaves slapping the furious wind.

late afternoon sun
shadowing the sun room wall
one green empty chair

This Spring

peppermint tree
delicate leaves cling
to the limbs

The peppermint was Ken's favorite tree. A number of upper limbs are still rotting. Squirrel's bee-shaped nest rests among green leaves.

One spring afternoon, when he and I were sitting on the deck, eating pizza, and watching squirrels chase one another through the grass, we decided to name the trees for certain people in our lives, mostly those who had died. He chose the peppermint for himself. He loved the way the trunk forked and leaned in two different directions.

Today after four months of blue silence, I hear him murmur through the boughs.

summer grasses—
all that remains
of warriors' dreams
　　　—Basho

Memorial Day, 2014

summer sun
bursting through the trees
clouds on the horizon

Unable to visit the cemetery, I sit on the deck, soak in some vitamin D, breathe into the new day. A downy woodpecker chips away at the sugar maple tree. A beetle on its back flails its legs. Flashes of metallic green.

my curious dog
paws a beetle
a hiss and a stink

When we were young, Mother tied strings around June bugs' legs, one bug each for my brother and me. Ignorant of our cruelty, we watched the bugs circle our heads, their bbbzzz-bbbzzz-bbbzzzing a favorite summer song.

Memorial Day
listening
to the silence

Through the Rain

Rain moves over the garden like thoughts of loss that race through my mind. It darkens the redwood fence. Fills the birdbath. Pours over the sides.

After so much sorrow, it's only natural to lose your way. To want to lie down and let the darkness embrace you. How many losses pile up before they start crowding your heart?

straight-down rain
how it pounds the ground
blinds the eye

Some days, when the sky turns and the trees whisper through the gray, you hear him in his study. He clears his throat. Fires up the computer. Or he walks down the hall, his soft-soled shoes gently stirring the air.

Then one morning you notice the buds on the honey locust. You feel the sun's rays. Your neighbor is planting a row of tomatoes. You warm your throat with a cup of tea. Give the dog and the cats a treat.

within the sweetness
of a sunlit tree
a cardinal chirrs

TWO

moments from a life

Prelude

birthcry!
      the stars
      are all in place
        -Raymond Roseliep

Ken arrives February 1, 1959, in the hush of a new day while most of Springfield sleeps. We drive to the hospital under glimmering sodium lamps which line the empty streets, the bare limbs of trees casting shadows across the sky. On the maternity ward, the dimly lit halls are filled with the breath of deep sleep.

His is a natural birth. A beautiful baby-blond hair, blue eyes, and a symmetrically-shaped head. He takes his formula and doesn't cry. Not like the two before him who had to be coaxed to eat and who shared their discomfort on a regular basis when they were wet or hungry. Later, as a toddler, when I try to nestle him in my lap, he noodles and squirms until his small teetering body slides onto the floor out of my arms.

sparrow singing—
its tiny mouth
open
      -Buson

moments from a life

Deserted

you've heard monkeys crying—
listen to this child
abandoned in the autumn wind
        -Bashoiki

In his first year Ken finds himself alone with his father and two older brothers. I am admitted to the psychiatric ward at St. John's Hospital for post-partum depression. I don't know how the family is getting along in my absence; I suspect not well, given that Forrest has never cared for the children. To him, they are a bother. They interfere with his reading *The New Yorker*, drinking Jack Daniels, watching Dan Rather on TV, working crossword puzzles. To avoid punishment for being too loud, they've learned to stay out of sight when he's around.

Shortly after I return home, we move to Indiana where Forrest goes to work at Purdue University as assistant to the head of the department of microbiology. We take temporary housing in the married students court on Airport Road. Ken entertains himself by standing on the wall heater in the boys' bedroom, peering out the window at rows of old army converted barracks, clothes flapping on the lines behind them, and aircraft which fly over day and night on their way to and from the airport. A fetching figure with his small hands clutching the window sill, his blue eyes peering from behind the window, the rest of his face hidden from view, his wet diaper slipping down to his knees.

She's put the child to sleep
and now she washes clothes
under the summer moon.
   - Issa

Lost

along with spring leaves
my child's teeth
are coming in
    -Kusatao Nakamura

Eighteen-month-old Kenny is clad only in a diaper when a motorist finds him running down Russell Street, his bare feet grabbing the hot pavement. With his rivulets of blond curly hair, eyes the color of forget-me-nots, the police think Kenny's a girl.

He'd slipped from his father's view, and attention, as his father surveyed the garden back of the house we'd just moved into on Russell Street.

Minutes later, we find him at the station sitting on an officer's desk, happily licking a lollypop. Just as happily, on the way home, on my lap, he finishes the lollypop, his two brothers watching from the back seat of the car.

coming back—
so many pathways
through the spring grass
    -Buson

Time Out

Quick, into the mist,
little bird,
you're free!
     -Oemaru

He hangs from a tall maple on Ball Hill Road, his legs
hugging a secure limb. He swings upside down, his
mouth turned upward in pleasure, his eyes swimming
with delight, reveling in the lightness he feels. He is in
another world, far from the insecurity and pain of being
the son of a father who shouts, hits his wife and
children, and a mother who cries and screams and
seems powerless to save him and his brothers.

His long blond hair forms a halo around his head. He
laughs at my fear he'll fall.

I catch
the maple leaf then
let it go
     -John Wills

Nature's Home

stillness—
piercing the rocks
the sound of cicadas
   - *Basho*

A thin moss covers the forest floor. The full moon shines on the tarp tent where Ken and his friend, Lee, spend the night, the taste of peanut butter and apples still on their tongues. Ken escapes the darkness of his life by drawing planes soaring, then exploding in the sky. Through dreaming of boats rocking on rising waves. A life of adventure, danger, excitement. A life of one's own that no one can enter. And no one can rip away.

drawing light
from another world—
the Milky Way
   -*Yatsuka Ishikara*

Celebration

children imitating cormorants
are even more wonderful
than cormorants
    -Issa

Nine-year-old Ken jumps into Scott's birthday snapshot, filling it with himself. He stands behind his brother, arms stretched, reaching for the candled birthday cake which Scott is shoving away from him at arm's length. Ken crosses his eyes, screws his mouth into a lopsided eight, scissors his arms up and down. It's a game. A pose. A snickering moment in an uneasy household.

Ken originally assigned himself the role as family comic to defuse the rising tension caused by his father's escalating anger. Now, he has incorporated the trait into his personality. Lost in his clown creation and feeding it to the rest of the world, he has erected a wall between himself and others. Between him and himself.

after the dancing
the wind in the pines
and the insects' cries
    -Sogetsu—Ni

Inconceivable

in this world
we walk on the roof of hell
gazing at flowers
  -Issa

On a hot summer evening on Ridge Road, when Ken is
fifteen, I'm in the kitchen washing the supper dishes
when I hear a commotion in the dining room. I look
through the door just in time to see Forrest hurl his iced
tea glass at Ken who is sitting at the table on his right.
Monopoly pieces, the glass, and ice cubes land on the
table and floor. Blood pours down Ken's face. I run for
a towel. Shout at Forrest to get the keys to the Mercury.

We head for St. Elizabeth ER, Ken and I in the back
seat, Forrest driving. The gaping wound on the top of
Ken's scalp bleeds profusely. I hold it together with the
towel which is soaking up fast. The blood runs onto his
tee shirt. He sits stiff and quiet next to me, his eyes wide
with fright.

clear stars
in the cold night
after the planes' roar
  -Hideno Ishibashi

The Price

In the afterglow of Gordon's embrace, I head for home. On the stereo, Helen Reddy sings, "I am woman, hear me roar..." I sing along.

On the Berlin Turnpike it rains. The windshield wipers squeak, fling streams of water into the darkness. Steam rises from the highway. I steer through a slippery wilderness, hold tight to the wheel.

When I enter the house, I find Forrest has fallen asleep on the couch holding an empty bottle of Jack Daniels. Always a fear, even as he sleeps. John and Scott are in their rooms. Ken, our teenaged son, stands at the gas range, his head bent, stirring a pot of spaghetti sauce. I'm startled by the image. He looks lost standing there. It should be me.

I break it off with Gordon. Promise the boys we'll leave Forrest as soon as I get my nursing degree.

thunder in his breath
mouth, fists, shoed feet
shattering the glow

The following spring, in the pale light of an early weekday morning, while the rest of us sleep, Ken climbs out his second floor bedroom window, descends the rose trellis, walks down the long driveway, and disappears. Only a note is left on his pillow. "Don't try to find me."

Resurrection

Saturday afternoon. I'm sweeping the carpet when the doorbell rings. Standing before me is the answer to months of prayers. My lost son!

"Ken! Come in!"

He follows me to the couch. Begins to sob. Tells of a breakup and coming off drugs. I hold him in my arms. He clings to me.

"Your room is ready," I say.

first light
everything in this room
was already here
       -Christopher Herold

The DJ

migrating birds—
fields of pampas grass
show the way
  -Kristen Deming

The first time I hear Ken's voice on the radio, I know he has it in him to be a winner. If he can just see, and own, his talent, he can go far. His voice is deep and smooth, and he has a dry wit that draws you in.

I've driven from West Hartford to Bristol in order to catch his very first show in his first paying job since he graduated from broadcasting school. I've parked by the side of the road not far from the station in order to get good reception on the car radio. It's Sunday morning, Mother's Day. I couldn't be prouder. And I'm so happy for him.

"Johnny Paycheck! 'Slide Off Your Satin Sheets.' This is for YOU, out there. You KNOW who you are," he says, in a seductive voice.

I know he's trying to sound cool. And he does. But I'm also aware that he is anxious. I won't let him know I'm listening, or recording. That would probably freak him out.

I place a tape in the record player on the seat next to me and push the 'on' button. I intend to record the entire show. And every one after that. When he was on the tele-auction in Springfield, Massachusetts, I got out my camera and took pictures of his credits on the television and of him on his rare appearances as a student.

I lean back into the seat, close my eyes, and listen. Paycheck's velvety voice massages the air, slides through the open window, and mixes with the trill of a sparrow in a field outside the car.

"You know where to find my door. I know what you're cry-ing for."

I remember when Ken came back home after a long absence. He was a lost soul. Broke, coming off drugs, he had no direction in life. All he wanted was a safe place to land. Just to survive. And a sympathetic ear. Broadcasting school changed all that. Now he has a purpose. Something he can work toward and feel good about. Something to which he can look forward.

Later, at home, I get an unexpected call. It's Ken! I can't believe it. He doesn't believe in 'special' days, I'm overcome, but I try not to show my excitement.

"Happy Mother's Day."
"Thank you," I say.

this world of dew
is yes, a world of dew
and yet...
     -Issa

32

Keeping Watch

The call comes before dawn. Ken's other lung has collapsed.

Two orderlies dressed in green wheel him back from surgery where his lung was repaired and inflated. He's asleep, connected to an IV, monitors for heart rate, blood pressure, and oxygen saturation, and a urine catheter. I adjust his covers, fluff his pillows, watch the rise and fall of his chest. I'm worried. This is the second collapse he's had in a year. I hope this time he'll stop smoking. I pick up a magazine, try to read. But the words are a blur. I place the magazine back on the window ledge.

hospital bed
in a straight chair
sitting close

sound of air
blood pressure cuff
filling and emptying

Ken stirs. Gazes at me through half-opened lids. "Oh!" He moans. "Get me some medicine!"

His eyes are wild with pain.

I run to the nurses' station. No one's around. The hall is quiet. Where is everyone?

I rush back to Ken's room. His moaning is louder, voice more urgent. I dash down the length of the hall, look for an open door, a nurse, a doctor, anyone who can help. Then I see her, a nurse behind a medicine cart leaving one room, about to enter the next.

"Please help," I plead. "My son. Ken Harrison. Just back from surgery. In pain. He needs an injection!"

"I'll be there," she says.

Relieved, I return to Ken. Wait for the medication, but still it doesn't come. I search for the nurse. She's nowhere in sight. Someone's behind the desk at the nurses' station. A secretary? I ask her to get my son's nurse.

"I'll be with you in a minute," she says.
"No! Now!" I scream. "Somebody help my son! He's in pain!"

spinning hoop
a fierce woman jumps through
a gentle woman

The nurse appears. I watch her open a cabinet, draw fluid from a vial into a syringe, push out the air bubbles. She follows me to Ken's room.

now he sleeps
breathing in
breathing out

afternoon sun
a fly sits motionless
on a window pane

on his blanket
prism'd sunbeams
dancing

THREE

"That's How I Roll"

Misquamicut Beach

Ken joins Forrest and me at our ocean-front rental. He stands in the doorway, unshaven, disheveled, holding a duffel bag, a six-pack of Colt 45, and a bottle of Beefeaters. He won't allow me to touch or hug him--a rule of his since he first left home at seventeen. It's been four years since he became estranged from us. I thought I might never see him again. He hasn't changed much. Tall, handsome, a fake look of arrogance in his large blue eyes. Behind the look, I see fear. And I see the courage which brought him here. In spite of needing a shave, he's a blessing, a wonderful sight, his appearance something I feared might not ever happen. Tired from working all night at Channel 3, he needs sleep more than anything, but he's too wired. He wants to take care of unfinished business with Forrest and put the past to rest.

Right away Ken pops a beer and begins to drink. The rest of the day he holds tightly to a can of the beer or a glass of gin, but the alcohol isn't strong enough to unlock his words. The long day is spent in small talk— "How is work? How about the weather? Nice beach." An uneasiness prevails, leaving the three of us edgy and tongue-tied.

In the evening, we sit by a window at a café and watch fishing boats come in. Ken orders Alfredo pasta but leaves it on the plate, untouched.

When we return from the café, Ken immediately goes to bed and falls asleep. I remove his boots and cover him with a blanket, then walk down to the water's edge. I collect seashells and driftwood for home and watch a fiery sky as the sun sets.

twilight sunset
bleeds into sky and water
how the seagulls rage!

Next morning, Ken nibbles on a piece of dry toast and crisp bacon in silence, then goes back to bed and sleeps.

Upon waking the second time, he tells us he's leaving. "I have to get up early and go back to work."

"But you were going to stay a week!" What changed his mind?

He shakes his head, gathers his duffel bag, and walks out the door.

As he strides down the drive, there's a sober air about him. He doesn't look back, doesn't see me standing on the deck, watching. But I sense he knows I'm there. He'll return to his secret address and unlisted phone number and I'll have no idea how to get in touch with him or know how he's doing. There's a small bit of comfort knowing where he works, but I wouldn't dare phone him there. Once, before he changed his phone number, when I called him at his apartment, he tried to have me arrested for stalking. And what if he changes jobs? As he drives away, I'm seized by a deep fear. What if I never see him again? He could be lost to me. Forever!

All day I pace through the rooms of the cottage. I go into the room where he slept the night before, study the surroundings, as if I look hard enough, I'll find him still there. I worry about his drinking. About his state of mind. He came to confront his father. And he lost his nerve. But maybe the fact that he came at all is a sign of hope.

That night, lost in the silence of Ken's absence, I wrap myself in a thin blanket, leave the cottage, and walk along the water's edge. The air is thick and smells of fish and seaweed. The moon is pale, the sky starless. As I approach the bottom of the hill, two lovers break away. The woman picks up her bag, and the two walk together, arms entwined, toward the Sandpiper Hotel. Farther down the beach, someone sits in a lifeguard's chair facing the horizon. I look out over the water, trying to find where the water ends and the sky begins. But there is no defining line. Only an endless spread of gray. For a moment I feel disoriented. As if I've walked to the edge of time. I gaze at the cottages behind me. They are still and empty. Only a few lights on. Boats that rocked on the water earlier are gone. Even the seagulls have disappeared. The night is still.

calm water
quieting the beach

quieting me

I return to the cottage and finally fall asleep. I dream about Ken. He is standing on a railroad track looking up at me as I watch him from the top of a hill. He is shouting something but I'm too far away to understand the words. He is unaware a train is bearing down on him at high speed. Terrified, I try to call out to him, but the words won't leave my mouth. I wake in a sweat.

outside the window
a seagull's screech
a rattle of wind

April, 1990

1

When Ken arrives, I'm making lasagna. His red Honda Civic shatters the gray evening as it whines up the driveway to the back of the house. Arms open, I run to meet him. Halfway there, I stop. Ken raises his arms, motioning for me to step back. His eyes are cold and empty.

"Keep your distance!"

I haven't seen him in two years, since he left Misquamicut Beach, suddenly, the day after he arrived. I want to touch him, to hug him, to tell him I love him, but I can only gaze at my tall, lanky son as if we were strangers. I watch with hungry eyes as he enters the house carrying a duffle bag and two six packs of Coors Lite, which he shoves into the refrigerator.

He begins to drink right away and continues all night as he confronts his father with the years of abuse he suffered at his hands. He stands over Forrest where he sits next to the fireplace, his face in Forrest's face like Forrest used to do to him.

"You ruined my life!" His eyes are wide and dark, his mouth twisted.

Forrest sits quietly in the gold Queen Anne chair by the fireplace, his arms thrown over the back, chest jutting out, a strange curve to his mouth, as if he's bracing himself for a verbal wallop, or worse, while trying to appear untouched by the words being thrown at him. At first I'm surprised he doesn't respond in anger, but then I see the fear in his eyes. Ken has finally found the strength to brave his father's anger. Neither Forrest nor I know what to expect.

"When I was seventeen you punched me and I fell to the ground. Remember? Do you remember the names you called me—stupid idiot, worthless piece of shit? All the times you hit and kicked and pulled me? Remember how you said I'd never amount to anything? How you'd break my arms if I didn't do what you said?"

Ken's voice breaks with emotion. He continues all night with a long list of grievances against Forrest. Occasionally he stops briefly and glares.

I lie awake all night wondering how Ken's visit will end. His anger is so fierce and deep, so raw, as if it all happened yesterday. Will he ever be able to put it behind him? I'm glad he's able to express himself at last, but I'm afraid Forrest will tire of being confronted and a bad scene will follow. My heart breaks for Ken because I know his words are not touching Forrest. But at least he's found his voice

Next day, Ken agrees to see our family therapist. But he won't ride with us. He takes his own car. At the therapist's office, Ken confronts Forrest again. Sitting on the edge of his seat, he shouts how his life has been filled with fear and how that fear has prevented him from living a satisfying life.

"I can't have a relationship," he says, glaring at Forrest. "I don't trust people."

When Forrest opens his mouth to speak, Ken points to him and shouts, "Be still! You never did let me speak. Well, now I'm going to. YOU sit and listen to ME! I've been saving this up for a long time."

On the way home, Ken stops for more beer and gin. He drinks all afternoon, but doesn't eat much. Just a little lasagna. He's still wound up. He paces and drinks and glares. I know Forrest deserves his wrath, but he's an old man now and I'm afraid for him. And I know that hitting Forrest won't make Ken feel better. I've stayed out of it because it's between the two of them, but Ken is full of alcohol and I'm not sure this is continuing to be a healing process.

"Ken..." I try to distract him. Isn't that what I always did in the past? Step in to get the heat off them?

"Be still!" Ken shouts. "This is between your husband and me." Ken refuses to recognize Forrest as his dad. I can understand why. But now Ken is drunk and he's just repeating himself. He points toward Forrest, walks toward him. Forrest stiffens in his chair.

"Ken, please sit down."

Ken glares at Forrest, then returns to the red leather chair by the window. Forrest's shoulders relax.

"Don't talk to your mother that way," he says, now that there's a comfortable distance between them.

It seems I'm just adding to the tension, so I go upstairs and sit on the radiator in my room, listening to what's happening downstairs and feeling my heart sink.

Next morning, Ken decides to drive to Dallas to see his brother, Chris.

"I'm glad he's gone. He's a silly boy," Forrest says."

"Really? You don't appreciate the fact that he drove 1200 miles to work things out with you?" "I didn't do anything wrong. He got what he deserved."

I feel sad for Ken. I'm glad he didn't hear what Forrest just said. I know he would like to think he accomplished something on this visit. That Forrest heard him, understood what he was trying to say, took some responsibility for the harm he did, and that he had some compassion. I fear that Forrest will never change,

After supper, I go into the guest room. Ken's bed is unmade. I don't have the heart to strip it. Will I ever see him again? I look around, walk from bed to dresser to chair. His spirit
permeates the room. It's almost as if he's in the room. I sit on the bed. Smooth the sheets and pillows. Rub the dresser top where he emptied his pockets. Lean back into the chair. His energy is intense. But it's not anger. It's more like grief...or despair. I have to leave the room. I can't breathe. Tears flood my eyes. I pace through the house. Room to room. Look out the windows at the street, now deserted. I try to will him

back. But of course I know he's gone. I find myself back in his room, feeling the emptiness, touching where he has been, trying to melt the knot in my chest.

April, 1990

2

About 8:00 PM, Ken calls. He says he's in Vineta, two and a half hours from Springfield. He wants to stay the night with us on his way back to Hartford. Another chance to work things out! Maybe I'll have a chance to talk with him this time. I'm deliriously happy!

I rush through the house, dusting, sweeping, and cleaning. I make a fresh bed for him, turn back the sheets, and switch on the soft lights next to his bed and the chair. I want the room to be inviting. Warm and comfortable. My heart begins to race. I can't get a deep breath. I wait in the foyer, sit on the radiator, watch for his red Honda.

When he arrives, the first thing he wants to know is if the beer and gin he left behind are still here. He finds them on the sun porch. He pours beer in a glass, adds ice cubes, and puts the rest in the freezer. He drinks while the three of us sit stiffly in the living room trying not to make waves. We talk about his visit with Chris, the weather, how long he expects it to take to drive back to Connecticut.

"I'm going to drive straight through," he says.

47

I'm worried about his driving 1200 miles without stopping to sleep. I want to tell him I'll pay for a motel if he'll spend the night somewhere. But I know I dare not.

"Do you know I used to do speed?"

Forrest and I both sense the question is more like a statement. It is evidently an opening for more confrontation. We both wait for what will come next. Ken turns to Forrest. He points to him.

"You're a coward," he says. "A bully and a coward."

Forrest doesn't reply. He seems to have had enough. He decides to go to bed. Says goodnight and walks upstairs. I'm glad. Ken has already had too much to drink. Another encounter would just be a repeat of the other night. Nothing would be accomplished. And it could escalate into something worse. Besides, I want to visit with Ken before he leaves.

But our talk turns out to be disastrous.

"I'm wired," Ken says. He paces through the living room, the dining room, the foyer. I can see he still has something on his mind.

Does he have issues with me? I want to know what they are. And what I can do to correct them.

"Well, for one thing, you acted like a victim in your dealings with your husband."

"I tried to protect you guys from him, Ken. When he was yelling, or hitting you, I'd scream for him to stop. I'd try to grab you from him. Often, then, he'd let you go and start in on me. But sometimes my attempts backfired. He'd hit you harder and tell you it was because I was interfering. I never knew which way it would go. Remember?"

"Well, why didn't you leave?" "I couldn't afford to, Ken."
I hate the tone of my voice. It sounds like I'm pleading. And I guess I am. I want him to understand my point of view. I need for him to believe I was a good mother. I need to believe it. Could I have done better? Should I have done differently? I don't know. Now Ken glares at me. I feel a chill.

"I didn't have a job. There weren't any shelters back then like there are today. Your grandparents wouldn't help. I had no place to go with four little boys."

It was true, but I often wonder if welfare would have been better than staying with Forrest. I worried about the neighborhoods we'd have to live in, the schools the boys would have to attend. They'd be in danger there, too. At least in our present situation, we knew what the danger was. Still, I feel guilty raising them in such a hostile and violent environment.

"You embarrassed me with your screaming," Ken says.

"I embarrassed myself, Ken. But sometimes screaming was the only way to get him to stop."

It's painful to be reminded. And to know how it made him feel. It must have made them all feel that way.

Ken goes to the kitchen, pours another beer over ice, returns and sits on the ottoman in front of the red leather chair facing me on the couch.

"You've broken my rules about touching and about calling on the phone."

"Ken, I haven't hugged you or put my hand on your shoulder, or even brushed up against you in the six years since you said not to. I've tried to respect your wishes. I haven't called you over three or four times."

He doesn't argue the point. His eyes are glazed. He seems to be having difficulty thinking. "John told me he calls you at work sometimes," I say.

"John has my permission. You don't." "Ken, why?"

"I've tried to tell you, but you're too stupid to understand."

He sounds as if he hates me. The ache in my gut spreads through my entire body.

He has insulted me on the phone quite a few times in the middle of the night after hours of drinking since he forbid me to call him. But I thought it was just the alcohol talking. Now I'm not so sure. He certainly doesn't respect me. He sounds just like his father.

50

"Ken, how can you talk to me like that? I'm not your enemy. I'm your mother. I love you." "I've told you not to say things like that."

He has, but sometimes I wonder if he doesn't need to hear it.

I think about the time I convinced Forrest to let him come back home after he got into trouble financially. How Forrest and I both took out loans so he could buy a pet store business, how he disappeared after it failed and left Forrest and me holding the bag. How I sent him to broadcasting school, paid all his bills, kept $20 bills in my jewelry box for him to take, without asking, when he needed cash. I remember the time he went cold-turkey off cocaine. He cried in my arms and I comforted him. How can he tear up my insides like this?

"Want me to leave?"

"No! I don't want you to leave. I just want to have the same rights you do. You won't allow me to call you. But you call me when you feel like it. You know where I live. I have no idea where you live. If I can't call you, you can't call me."

"Fine!" he says.

At once I wonder, what have I done? I worry now that he'll stop calling me and I'll have no contact with him at all, even if it is only after he's been drinking. At least I've had some assurance he's still okay.

"After you told us you were disowning us, it was hard, but I was finally accepting it. Then you resurrected yourself, saying you wanted to put the past behind us. Well, it seems you came just to get things off your chest, and to torture us in the process."

I'm angry with Ken now, for his disregard for my feelings. And with Forrest for all the harm he did. With myself for being so weak. It looks hopeless. None of us will change. I want to cry. Instead, I get up from the couch, walk over to the end table by Ken's chair, scoop a picture of him into an open drawer and bang the drawer shut. I can't believe what I'm doing. It's like watching a bad movie. This isn't what I want to do. I want to grab him, hold him, and tell him I love him. I want to beg him to come back into my life.

"Why not put it in a harder place to get to?" Ken's voice is low. He chokes on the words. "I'm going to bed, Ken. We both need sleep."

Shortly, I hear him go into the bathroom. Soon afterwards, the front door closes. I rush down the stairs in time to see his Honda back down the drive and shriek into the dark. I watch from the foyer widow. I want to run after him. He's in no condition to drive. What if he has an accident? What if he is hurt or is killed! Or arrested and jailed in a strange town? I walk into the living room, take his picture out of the drawer, rock back and forth, holding it to my chest, the sound of screeching tires still in my ears. I pray that he'll see that he is in no position to drive, that he'll turn around and come back. I sit for a long time, looking up and down the empty street, waiting for the sound of his car. But I see only soft pools of light cast by the sodium lamps lining the street. The street never looked so empty. Finally, I realize he's not going to return. The lump in my throat grows larger. I hope he makes it safely to Connecticut. But I know, even if I see or talk with him again, what both of us really want to say will never get said and will be stuck in our throats forever. I creep upstairs to my bed, still holding onto Ken's picture. The clock on the mantle chimes loudly in my ears.

Remembering July, 1972

In the dark of night

he got the boys out of bed, said
come into the living room,

he had something

important to say,

made them sit facing me,

their eyes blurred from sleep,
their pajamas twisted.
Your mother's a whore, he said.
They remained silent,
just looked at the floor,
played their part in this drama

instinctively. Tonight
he wanted only their ears.
I, too, was quiet, out of fear.

Could they ever know
how starved a woman can become
for a touch that doesn't bruise,
but soothes,

for words sweet,

not crushing, nor demeaning;
how very desperate

a woman can become for love,

she'll willingly drive sixty miles
to a ghetto in New Haven
where a drinking man waits
and hopes in his bed
ready to hold her in arms
as warm as his eyes;

where, outside his door, people spill
their guts on the street,

have their legs broken—

or maybe aren't that lucky;
how even the outer turmoil

is lost in a hunger

so strong

it will push her to risk everything

How could I tell them how it could happen? Tell them
so they'd understand? Tell them

my thoughts weren't with them?

How could I?

A Call From My Son

He tells me this is the end,
not to try and reach him, then
he hangs up the receiver
before I'm ready
to say goodbye.
From the kitchen window
I watch
a late autumn storm.
Wind chokes the garden,
turns cone flowers
and black-eyed susans
inside out,
and whips the birch
to the ground.
Rolling clouds darken.
A wet-winged bird on a shaky wire
tries to hold on.

For Ken

Sometimes when I stand in your room and remember
how you arranged the furniture,

I search for a success
I want to have had with you.

It's been four years since your red Honda
shrieked out of the drive, headlights piercing
the dark.

My son, I often think I see you
in other bodies, other souls—
young men
looking moving talking
like you
at Trotter's restaurant,
Battlefield Mall,
speeding down Sunshine.

I have to stop myself from calling after them.

FOUR

moments from a life

My Son, a Stranger

stifling August
two sparrows on a curb
widening their beaks

At Ruby Tuesday's, we sit in a booth facing each other. Ken drinks Irish whiskey; I sip decaf coffee. I haven't seen him or spoken with him in ten years. He's in Springfield only to attend a service for Scott, his brother who committed suicide. He agreed to see me only if I came alone. He looks much the same—a tall, lanky young man with thick brown hair and a sober expression. In his dark suit, he shifts uncomfortably, voice stiff and guarded.

He tells me he's been married for three years and is in the process of getting a divorce. He works at a Hartford TV station and lives with his cat at his home in Coventry.

As we move to leave, I wonder if I'll ever see him again. He grabs a napkin from the dispenser, writes his address and phone number, hands it to me.

"Don't share this with anyone. Especially 'your husband' (speaking of his abusive father). I don't want to see or hear from him again."

I take the napkin, a white paper square, thin and fragile, my eyes embracing the familiar handwriting. I spread the napkin on the table, smooth its corners, fold it back into a square. Carefully, I place it into my handbag.

my long lost son...
having said all we can say
still, we linger

New Directions

Three months after Forrest dies, I move to Connecticut to be near Chris and Ken, my sons. Nikki and Jeti, my two miniature poodles, come with me. We stay with Ken in Bristol. I am 80 years old and trying to adjust to being single after 59 years of marriage. Ken has been divorced for seven years after a three-year marriage to someone I don't know and never met. It's a new adventure for both of us.

It doesn't take long for us to settle into a routine. Ken sleeps mornings and works afternoons and evenings. I spend my time grocery shopping, cooking, reading, unpacking my belongings, and taking care of the dogs. I hire Pooper-Scoopers to clean up after the dogs in the pint-sized yard behind the condo. When it snows, Ken shovels the steps and part of the yard so they can go out.

When we're both free at the same time, we sit in the living room and talk about our lives. Ken shares work events, his plans for making money and moving into a larger house. He shows me his ever-growing coin collection. Sometimes we order pizza or Chinese. These are my favorite times. I can't forget how it used to be. We were all together as a family, though not a happy one. Then Ken was out of our lives. And now he and I are together again.

On Christmas Day, I'm attacked by a bullmastiff. The injury is on the back of my upper arm—hard for me to get to, or see. Ken takes me to weekly doctor appointments and helps with the daily cleaning and medicating of the wound and the changing of bandages for the months it takes me to mend. When I ask if he will help me with it, he says, "I have the technology." It's his favorite response when I ask for help. His way of saying "yes."

That winter we both come down with the flu, followed by pneumonia. We take turns going to the drugstore for medicine and bringing ginger ale and crackers upstairs. Ken fills a steamer to moisten the air around my bed. Eventually, we both heal.

I had hoped to have the opportunity to make amends for mistakes I made in the past. But it's difficult for me to climb the stairs with my arthritic knees. However, it is the emptiness and loneliness of Ken's condo which finally overcomes me. My upstairs bedroom, where I spend most of my time, looks out onto a woods. The front of the condo has no windows. I don't know anyone in Bristol. I feel cut off from the world. Also, Ken has sudden outbursts, usually when

he's frustrated with me. His verbal attacks always take me by surprise and leave me puzzled, frightened, and sick at heart. The uncertainty of not knowing when, or over what, Ken will become angry, keeps me anxious and withdrawn.

After seven months, I decide to go back to Springfield, which is familiar, and more comfortable. So I pack my belongings, and Ken drives me the 1200 miles to my new home.

"You can always come back if you change your mind," he says.

The way it turns out, two years later he comes to live with me.

violets here and there
in the ruins
of my burnt house
  -Shokyu-ni

Mysterious Squirrel

At the foot of my bed this morning, I found the cats' toy
    squirrel.
Lying on its belly, chestnut fur soft and fluffy,
    I knew the cats hadn't tossed it there—
it had been placed too carefully

Later, it clung to Ken's coffee maker, its tail and ears
    drooping, as though
it had had too much to drink.
Next, it had moved to the kitchen counter, checking out
    the burners on the stove.

I decided two could play this game.

It made its way to Ken's desk, settled near his keyboard,
    then leaped
to the hallway floor along with a kitty dancer and a
    feather toy.

Now it sits in Ken's recliner next to mine.
Always it moves in secret.

When no one's watching, the cats' toy squirrel pops up
    where we least expect to find it,
reminding me of other times when I turn my back in the
    kitchen, food on my plate disappears, or

the entire plate does. Sometimes a pan of lasagna or
   chocolate banana bread seems to take flight.
Then, just as mysteriously, the food reappears.

Ken and I have been through rough years together—
   estrangement, anger,
late night whiskey phone calls. Our being able to live
   together was a long time coming.
It's been two years, and this squirrel has seen us
   through.

"And the body, what about the body?"
    -Jane Kenyon

Ken told me many times how he would live to be 700 years old. He would have all his organs replaced. He'd be a bionic man. It was another one of his grandiose plans. I don't know if he truly believed he could accomplish such a feat or if it was a fantasy he was sharing.

Ken had abused his body for years. Each of his lungs collapsed due to his heavy smoking. For the second lung, he needed surgery to keep it in place. Merely inflating it didn't work. In spite of his lung problems, Ken kept on smoking for quite a few years after the collapses. His breathing was impaired. I noticed it when he tried to play a piece on his saxophone (which he nicknamed 'vapor') for Forrest and me when we visited him one summer.

He drank alcohol to excess on a regular basis, smoked pot, and probably did street drugs as well. His diet consisted mostly of fast foods. He had surgery on his legs which he said were unaligned from birth, affecting his gait and causing pain. I'm not sure if the surgery helped him at all, though he said it did.

Not long after the surgery, his knees began to hurt. The doctor said he needed knee replacements but wanted to wait to do that until Ken was older. He kept odd hours, often stayed up all night, developed insomnia. He was prescribed medication for bipolar disorder. Sometimes he stopped taking it, but always had to start up again after he became increasingly depressed, or hyper. He

72

had two mild strokes. The doctors found a hole in his heart, which was probably genetic.

After he left his job at ESPN and came to live with me, he complained that something was affecting his concentration and his memory. He suffered from attention deficit disorder and the insomnia became increasingly worse. I bought him a CPAP machine to help him breathe at night. All of his conditions were worsening, in spite of a team of doctors and numerous tests. He even participated in a study which necessitated he undergo surgery for an implant near his heart.

Ken had big plans. He was extremely intelligent and was excited about executing his ideas. But his health got in the way. And, yes, he abused his body. He was dealing with his problems the best way he knew how. I suspect he did come into the world with some of them. Genetics can be hard to overcome.

Six months ago, when Ken left for the last time, he was in a rage. But his eyes were filled with fear and pleading. "I'm dying," he said.

bionic implant
would that one could replace
a broken heart

Mercy ER Waiting Room,
With Ken

Cold darkness, ceiling lights dim
in the long night hours. Figures come and go.
They wait and watch, chairs arranged
in groups of strangers.

A child in pajamas hangs limp
on his mother's shoulder; beyond
a man in overalls cradles
his bloody hand. The woman asleep
 beneath a sheet could be dead.
I'm in a wheelchair and I shiver
in my blue chambray jumper,
my knit sweater coat.

A family sitting next to me
laughs, mocks,…chills my bones,
like your eyes, uncaring, and
now closed.

Ken and Chris

After eight years of being estranged from his brother, Chris, and two months before his own death, Ken decides he wants to have a relationship with Chris. I'm not sure what brought him to this decision. I've been reminding him that after I'm gone, Chris will be the only family he'll have left. But I don't think that's what changed his mind. Perhaps he realizes his expectations of others is often unreasonable. Maybe his and Chris's common interest in the computer brought them together. Or he's discovered he loves his brother. More than likely, it's a combination of these things. Whatever the reason, it's something I feared would never happen. It's cause for celebration.

The two of them text and talk on the phone for several weeks after Ken's initial phone call. Then Chris drives from Ellington, Connecticut to Springfield, Missouri for a week's visit. He takes my bedroom, and I sleep on my recliner in the sun room with Jenny, my poodle girl. Since I'm not able to cook for visitors, we eat, mostly, from restaurants. I call in the orders and the boys pick them up: chicken pot pie and salmon croquettes with creamed peas from Heritage Cafeteria, pasta and salads from The Olive Garden, sandwiches and soups from Nearly Famous Deli, Chinese food from Mr. Yen's, steak burgers from Steak and Shake. One night Ken and

Chris eat tandoori at Gem of India, their favorite Indian restaurant.

They spend most of their time in Ken's office in front of his computer at his desk. It's as if they've never been apart. They laugh and they talk and they plan. They drink beer and wine, eat pizza, and rehash their lives. They dream of doing business together. A glow spreads through the house.

After Chris leaves, Ken shares with me a hope he has about Chris moving to Springfield. He says he's willing to give up his office so Chris can have a room of his own. Then, after I'm gone, he and Chris will go on living in the house and doing business together. I remind him that Chris is living with his girlfriend in Connecticut, and I don't see that happening. But Ken is fairly confident, as he always is with his ideas, that his dream will come true.

I'm just happy we're finally a family again. The three of us who are left.

the vast night—
now nothing left
but the fragrance
　　　-Jorge Luis Borges

Last Hours

all day Christmas
mother and grown son   apart
separate rooms

The morning after Christmas I find Jenny, my poodle, locked in a crate in Ken's bedroom. He had put her there because he found her eating the cat's food. I open the latch. She jumps into my arms.

"Can we talk about where we can move the kibble so she can't get into it?" I ask. He refuses. Prefers to teach her through punishment. I don't argue. I can see he's agitated. He begins to shout, his voice loud and high, in a tone that makes me feel I'd better leave. I roll my wheelchair down the hall. Quickly. He follows, shouting all the while, his body bent so that his face is close to mine. So close I can feel his breath. When I've almost reached my bedroom, he turns abruptly, dashes into his study, bangs the door until it comes off its hinges.

hot breath
a fire outside the fire
of winter

thunder in his voice
two cats race down the hall
shoulder to shoulder

77

disturbed by the storm
underneath the futon
my wide-eyed poodle

Later, in the sunroom, Susie, my niece, here to do laundry and other chores, tries to coax Jenny from under the futon. Ken walks in. Sits in the green recliner next to mine.

"You're going to outlast us all," he shouts. "You're too stubborn to die." He's so filled with rage, I'm afraid he'll have a stroke.

"You're going to kill yourself with your anger, Ken."

"Thirty thousand dollars. I'll leave for thirty thousand dollars."

I don't want him to leave. I'm familiar with his outbursts. He has threatened to leave before. But this time it's different. Instead of cooling off, his anger keeps escalating. I'm uneasy. So I call my financial agent.

"They say it'll take a week to get the money," I tell him.

He leaves the room, paces through the house, returns several times. Finally tells Susie to leave. "Two hours. Give me two hours. I want to talk to her. Alone!"

She refuses to leave.

"If she doesn't leave," he says to me, "I will."

I don't ask her to go. In his present frame of mind, I'm afraid to be alone with him.

He goes to his room, starts packing. In and out of the house, filling the car with his belongings. Comes into the sun room and hands me the key to his blue Liberty. "I'm going to take the Buick."

As he makes his last trip to the Buick, I roll my chair to the kitchen which he has to pass on his way out of the house. I want to tell him I love him, but I know it's not allowed. I call to him just before the door closes, "Be careful!"

leaving with suitcase
into the long night
his anger follows

storm over
in the now quiet house
the heavy air lifts

the animals creep
out of hiding
stunned silence

Winter, 2013

mercurial sky
an unraveled robin's nest
slips to the ground

The funeral director advises me not to view the body. "I wouldn't want my mother to see," he says. I can't help but wonder, did his eyes shatter? Did he blow away his brains? Does he still have a face? What I can imagine is probably worse than what I might see.

My last image of him is one of a stranger. Not the living son I thought I knew. He left the house four days ago in a rage. His eyes wide and wild, face brick-red, voice so jarring the dog and cats ran for cover. How could anyone survive such fury? "Be careful," I called after him.

In my mind, he is the blond, blue-eyed boy who collected stamps, fed his angelfish and mollies, loved to walk through the woods with his brother. He liked spaghetti, pizza, and Dunkin' donuts. He was 53.

his hungry cats
I place his ashes
on the mantel

FIVE

moments from a life

This Time of Day

shadows lace
the peppermint tree
back of the house
the squirrels' nest
in darkness

The hours between sunlight and nightfall. Between gleaming and gloom. Shadows from the trees sweep the fence. Each slat exposed in the still air.

I watch as the sun weakens its grip. Grief stretches from the trees to the fence. There's an eerie silence. Tree limbs empty of birds. The glare on the fence pales. Shadows deepen, cover the slats, one by one, until only a few ghosts remain.

And now, the last one has faded and finally disappeared. Like a light extinguished. All in dark-ness. Where have the days gone? Work. Play. Thoughts. Desires. Swallowed by night. Only ashes remain. The weight of it squeezes my throat. Sorrow seeps through.

It's been thirteen years since Scott took a gun and filled his bedroom with blood, eleven years since colon cancer squeezed the life from John, six years since the rattle in Forrest's throat stilled him forever, seven months since Ken took his life in a hotel room.

in the pause
between daylight and darkness
they die again
and I
along with them

A New Old Grief: What Mother Wants to Remember the Death of Her Child?

Scott's happened in August when the sun was fierce and
the air stood still. Grass burned and lakes dried out,
and he no longer wanted to live.

John's, in February, after a short illness,
an ice storm froze flowers: bent, broken,
they lay on the ground, mourners' footprints
covered by ice, the earth unmoving.

Ken died in December the night following Christmas
alone in a motel room. After five sleepless nights
in a psychotic rage, he couldn't see a way out.

Birthdays, 4th of July, Christmas, and then Easter…
other holidays. Every month a cause for grief.
And I ask myself, is this why I'm here—

to guide and love and cherish, to watch them die
before they have a chance to live,
to let them go before my own life ends?

85

summer gray squirrels
have emptied the bird feeder
these black sunflower seeds
from high in the maple tree
the Ooo of a mourning dove

morning darkness comes
as I wake from dreams of him
struggling to breathe
remembering how he labored
to inflate his ailing chest

in the lonely room
laptop computer
iPhone and the gun he used
weapons to stop the haunting
words from a former work crew

I move his ashes
to grandmother's wooden chest
next to the others...
watching a lost butterfly
miss a nearby nectar

Selling Ken's Jeep

in the blue silence
beneath the peppermint tree
a cardinal feeds

I sit in my wheelchair at the back of the garage and watch two men in the driveway. They are inspecting Ken's jeep. The younger man fingers the tires; the gray-haired one opens the door on the driver's side and checks the gas gauge. The dark blue paint has been washed and shined. It shimmers in the afternoon sun. The image fills my eyes.

The jeep has been in the driveway since Ken died, almost a year ago. It's on the other side of the Park Avenue. When Chris was here on vacation, I asked him to move it there so I couldn't see it from my living room window. The sight of it still causes me to catch my breath. The cars won't fit in the garage since Ken's belongings take up all the space.

The older man nods, says something to Mark, my hairdresser's husband, who is selling the jeep for me.

Mark walks back to where I sit.

"They're interested," he says. "They're good people. The older man lives in Ash Grove. He's the boy's

88

grandfather and he's buying the jeep for his grandson. They want to know if you'll come down on the price. I told them I didn't think so."

I don't respond. I almost hope the price will prohibit them from buying the vehicle. Ken was proud of that jeep. He nursed it like it was his child. He drove me to my doctor appointments in it. It was a part of him. And now it's a part of me. But I don't want to leave it out in the weather another year, though I can't imagine it not being there. No one but Ken should be driving his jeep. I try to envision the driveway without the jeep in it. A wave of anxiety fills my chest.

Mark returns to the men. They say a few words. I watch as the older man reaches into his pocket, pulls out an envelope and hands Mark a pile of bills. Mark gives him the title to the car. The older man opens the door on the driver's side and sits behind the wheel. The young man opens the passenger door and is about to slide in when I call to him. I'm not ready for the jeep to go yet. I need to know it's in good hands. That it will be treated well. I want to know more about the person who will be driving it.

"What's your name?"

The boy walks back to where I sit. He smiles and extends his hand.

"My name is Charles. Charles Dunlap. I'm a medical student at Columbia University. I just got married two months ago."

"I hope you enjoy the car."

"Thank you," he says. "I'll take good care of it."

I like him. He's polite and kind. He'll be a good doctor. If anyone has to have the jeep, I'm glad it's him.

I watch the jeep as it backs out of the driveway, turns down Cragmont, and disappears. I imagine Ken behind the wheel. He's going to school. Or the post office. Or the drugstore. He'll be back soon. I'll hear the car door slam before he walks into the house. He'll go into his office and open his computer. Cleo, his cat, will nestle herself onto the back of his chair. Niles, his other cat, will curl up on a folded blanket in a book shelf behind him. He'll be there when I go to sleep. He'll still be there when I wake in the morning.

But wait! No! The picture breaks into fragments.The pieces zigzag through my mind like bits of an unfinished jigsaw puzzle crashing through the air. Ken's bedroom is still here. But the bed is not the way he left it—covers bunched up, pillows on the floor. It's freshly made with a clean spread, pillows stacked neatly at the head. His computer is gone from his office. The desktop is bare. The cat boxes have been moved from his bathroom to a corner by the office window. His black western hat rests on the top bookshelf where his camera and equipment used to be. Ken's clothes are collecting dust in the closet. His tall amethyst geodes line the walls of both rooms.

But his jeep won't be back. And neither will Ken! I sit for a few minutes turning those two thoughts over in my head.

I'm trying to reorient myself when Mark appears with a pile of $100 dollar bills. I hold them in my left hand, finger them with my right. They cramp my hand with their thickness. I turn each by its corner, like pages in a book. I don't like the feel of them. Some are wrinkled, others dirty and smooth. The new ones are stiff. I want to drop them. All of them, to the floor. I want them out of my sight. I count out four bills and hand them to Mark. I slip the rest into my shoulder bag.

After Mark leaves, I sit for a while longer fixing my eyes on the empty spot next to the Buick. In a nearby blue spruce, a cardinal chirrs.

autumn dusk
in the driveway
silence spreads

After

Waking in the middle of the night in my (old) room, I think of you. Why, tonight, is your absence so painful? Is it your cats who sleep so peacefully next to my dog on the bed? Or the house too dark and quiet? When you were here, your room was lit up all night; you were in it, sitting in front of your computer. Sometimes I'd hear your footsteps in the hall as you walked to the bathroom. Or to the kitchen for a snack or a late meal.

I remember the day you arrived. You were so physically compromised, you could no longer work. So you left your job at ESPN, sold your condo in Connecticut, and drove to Missouri to live with me. We agreed it was a good arrangement for both of us. You needed a place to stay and I wanted to be at home rather than live in a facility. You drove me to my doctor appointments, ran errands, took out the trash, picked up the mail and whatever else needed to be done that I couldn't do. I provided a place for you to live and I paid the bills. Both of us expressed our gratitude that we were there for the other. Sometimes we talked about our partnership being part of a divine plan.

It was an evening in late October when you finally arrived. You were smiling. You'd been driving for two days, but you didn't seem tired. I'd been waiting for you for hours, watching from the sunroom window vehicles passing on Luster, headlights beaming in one direction or the other. I couldn't determine the color of the cars, but I could make out their shape and height. Many times I mistakenly took other vehicles for your blue Liberty jeep.

Disappointment and anxiety rose in me when I realized it wasn't you. I was glad when you were finally safe, at home. "How can you be so alert," I asked, "after such a long drive?"

"That's how I roll," you said, with a smile. That phrase became your favorite way of explaining yourself.

Our arrangement seemed to work perfectly. I took the master bedroom with bath and you took the other two bedrooms, your bathroom the one off the hall. I had your bedroom ready with your dad's sleigh bed and matching chifferobe, a table and a lamp. The other room was your study, and you were bringing your office furniture. We shared the rest of the house. We were a family.

At first we ate our meals together. I cooked the main meal at noon because it's healthier to eat lighter in the evening, but our schedules were so different, with you up at night and sleeping during the day. So I continued to cook at noon and you warmed up leftovers when you felt hungry. I never told you this, but I missed your company at meal times. I enjoyed the days you picked up food and we ate together in the sunroom, making conversation and treating the animals with an occasional bite. Saturday was 'pizza' day. I ordered them from Dominos. You always had pepperoni, sausage, onions, and hot peppers on yours. I had a veggie.

The pizza was good, but it was the conversation I looked forward to. We talked about everything—religion, politics, our health, the pets, current events, our family history, plans for the future. One of your plans was to live forever. "I'll be a bionic man," you said.

Oh, how I miss you. Especially at night when I see a set of headlights approaching on Luster, when the walls squeak and groan, or when the covers on your bed swell into a small hill where Niles, your male cat, lies underneath where you used to sleep. Sometimes it seems he's still waiting for you.

circling light
two curled up cats
touching noses

calico cat
room to room
follows the sun

morning dew
burning bush sheds
red jewels

red streaks
in the maple tree
two cardinals pass

in the shimmering haze
the red poodle
spinning, spinning, spinning

SIX

moments from a life

My dear son, Ken,

It's been a year since the day after Christmas and you made that dreadful decision to end your life. It's hard sometimes to believe you're really gone. I still feel your presence in the house. I smell your aftershave. I hear you shuffling papers in your office or walking into the kitchen for a cup of coffee. I imagine you asleep in your bed, your breath filling the room. Sometimes, it seems, you clear your throat, or cough, or mumble something to one of the cats. Once in a while I sense the garage door opening and closing, as if you're returning home after running errands. My ears fill with the music of your sounds.

"Do you want anything from Springfield?" you'd ask, before you left to go into town.

It was your way of saying that anywhere in town was not too far for you to go. It was a private joke between us because I didn't like to ask you to pick up my meds or mail a letter or stop at the bank unless it was near where you were going.

You were finally calling me Mom. And you even accepted an occasional hug. But I was not allowed to say "I love you" or anything remotely related to such a sentiment.

Today the world is gray. I sit in the sunroom in my green recliner next to your empty one near the window, look out at the frozen ground, and remember warmer days. The trees are minus their leaves and the birds which roosted on their limbs. Even the squirrels seem to have disappeared. And you, my son, whose absence screams at me, "Where is he?"

You and I should be eating our Saturday pizzas. Treating Nikki and Jeti, the old dogs, with bits of the crust. Plotting a comic strip you were going to write about them: Jeti was to be named Noodles because of how she went limp when you picked her up; Nikki was to be Snapper because she growled and snapped at Jeti when Jeti overstepped her boundaries. We had many a laugh watching those dogs and planning how you were going to portray them.

We compared notes on the three TV shows we both watched—*Big Brother, The Office,* and *Curb Your Enthusiasm.* You introduced me to the last two. I watched them only to give us something to share.

We talked about your plans to make a lot of money and move into a mansion. You said a wing of the mansion would be for me. You were going to become a world traveler and you would buy gems for a holistic shop you were preparing to open.

You filled your two rooms with healing crystals and tall amethyst geodes, almost as tall as you. I haven't been able to burn the Blue Pearl sandalwood incense since you died. Or clear the rooms of bad vibrations with feather and sage in an abalone shell. That was your thing, a ritual you performed when we felt one of us, or the house, needed to be cleansed.

100

You didn't have the chance to follow your dreams. Your travel was limited to this country, where you vacationed on East Coast shores and ski resorts in Colorado. You had a good job at ESPN but didn't work long enough to accumulate enough funds to own a business, live in a mansion, or become a world traveler. You never found time to write that comic strip. You'd become a physical and mental wreck. You needed new knees. You couldn't finish a sentence without struggling for breath. You had a hole in your heart and hypertension. You had had two mild strokes. You were also battling bipolar disease and attention deficit disorder. But you never stopped trying to overcome your challenges. You were brave. And fearless. I admire your tenacity.

In spite of your being a full-time student and having to deal with physical and mental problems, you drove me to my doctor appointments, emptied the trash, got the mail, and ran errands. You went for job interviews, but no one ever called you back. Your life was difficult, to say the least. I can only imagine what mental anguish and physical torture brought you to the decision that stole you from your brother, Chris, and me forever.

I remember we often talked about the afterlife. You believed we chose to come here to earth in order to evolve, that we selected our parents, and we continued to return to earth until we were completely evolved. At the same time, you said you planned on living forever. You would have all your organs replaced. You would be a bionic man. But if by some chance you did die, you would send me a sign from the other side. You didn't say what the sign would be, but some of the things that have happened since you died make me wonder. I hear strange noises at night. I find drawers and cabinet doors open, clothes and other items strewn across the floor. Just days after I collected your belongings from the police department, I found your gun and cell phone lying on the floor. I had placed them in the back of a cabinet behind stacks of books. The strange part was, the books were not disturbed. How did the gun and the phone get past the books without them being moved? And who removed them from the cabinet? I wanted to blame the cats. But they had never done anything like that before. Not to mention that the gun was too heavy for them to move. Was it you, Ken? If so, what was the message?

Do you remember the Christmas I paid to have a star named for you? You were a good astrologist and you said sometimes you felt you were from another planet. Now, when I see a blinking star, I imagine it's you sending messages to me. Letting me know you're happy and at peace.

You were so brilliant and creative, but your illness, insomnia, and the wrong medicines filled you with fear and rage. You died in a strange place, alone, without comfort or compassion. I'm so sorry I didn't recognize how ill you were or know what to do for you. It's sad that you were unable to share your pain. Doing so might have saved your life.

When you left the house, I could only feel relief, as I feared for my own safety. I had no idea of the demons which haunted you or that you were on a path of no return. Forgive me for not being aware, for not being able to save you.

Wherever you are, I hope you've found peace. That you are filled with joy and happiness. And you have a strong body that is comfortable and takes you anywhere you want to go. And I hope you have found that mansion in the sky where you will have all the room you need to be authentic and whole and to explore the meaning of your life, where you will find beauty and joy and the love you so desperately needed but were unable to accept when you were alive.

I wish, when you were alive, you could have allowed me to share with you what a treasure you were, how proud I was of you, and how very much I love you. I told you how sorry I was about your entire life and my part in it. But I'm not sure you believed me or that you forgave me. I speak to you now in silent anguish. You have joined your two brothers in the vault of my heart. Each one of you has taken a large piece of me with you. I am struggling to be whoever I am with what is left without you. Just know that I miss you very much and hope that you have found relief from the pain you experienced in your life.

Rest in peace, my precious son.

summer evening—
the chatter of birds
in the junipers

summer dusk
drumming the lampshade
thin-winged moths

About the Author

Mary Harrison, is a retired psychiatric nurse practitioner who spends her time writing poetry and prose. She lives in Springfield, Missouri with her miniature poodle, Jenny, and two cats, Niles and Cleo. Some of her poems have appeared in the *Kansas Quarterly, Midwest Poetry Review, Mediphors, Poetry Motel, Kota Press Poetry Journal, Reflections*, and other small presses and literary journals. She is the author of three previous volumes: *Unforeseen, And You Will Know the World's Name*, and *Beneath Our Feet*.

www.ingramcontent.com/pod-product-compliance
Lightning Source LLC
Chambersburg PA
CBHW050411290526
45786CB00003B/1213